The Life
of
Moses

The Life
of
Moses

James Beaton

Illustrations
Catherine Miller Ellis

Cover Design
Brian Hegney

Christian Focus Publications

Published by
Christian Focus Publications
Geanies House,
Fearn, Tain,
Ross-shire IV20 1TW
Scotland

© 1986 Christian Focus Publications

ISBN 0 906731 50 X

Typeset in Scotland by John G. Eccles Printers Ltd, Inverness
Printed in England by Cox & Wyman

List of Illustrations

Contents

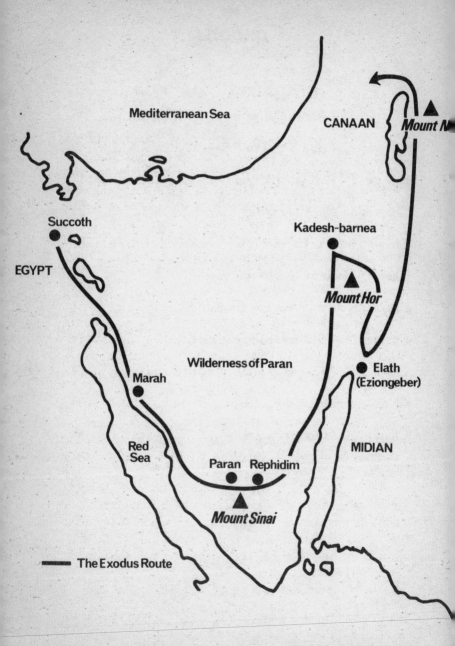

The route to the Promised Land.

CHAPTER 1

From Slave to Prince

Moses was born in Egypt at a time when the king of that country had just passed a law which threatened the lives of all Hebrew baby boys. To us it seems a strange time for Moses, the great leader of the Hebrews, to have been born but God does everything according to his plans which are always for the best in spite of our doubts.

Pharaoh, king of Egypt, had decided that every male child born to Hebrew parents was to be drowned. This evil law was passed because Pharaoh was afraid of the Hebrews. They were a strong, healthy people and their numbers had greatly increased since their arrival in Egypt.

When the Hebrews had first come to Egypt they had been welcomed as friends of the Egyptians. One of their own people, Joseph, had been given a very important job to do and was highly thought of by everyone including the king of Egypt. But now many years later the Hebrew people were treated like slaves and Pharaoh showed them little or no kindness. He was afraid that if any of his enemies were to attack him the whole Hebrew nation would join them and Pharaoh and his people would be defeated.

So Pharaoh's plan was to get the numbers of the Hebrews down. At first he thought that by making life as difficult as possible for them by overworking them the numbers of the Hebrews would decrease. But Pharaoh was to be disappointed. The Hebrew people became even more numerous.

His next plan was to try to get the help of the nurses or midwives who were present at the births of the children. Pharaoh told them that when they were helping a Hebrew

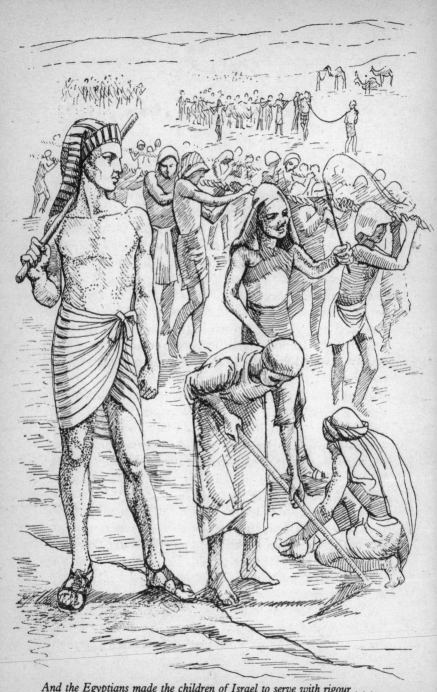

And the Egyptians made the children of Israel to serve with rigour . . .
(Exodus 1, v.13).

woman to give birth if the child was a boy they should kill him, but if a girl, they could let her live.

The two Hebrew midwives believed in God and they knew that God would be angry if they did as Pharaoh had told them so they allowed all the baby boys to live. We should remember that it is far more important to obey God than to obey man. The Bible tells us the names of these two brave women. They were called Shiphrah and Puah.

Naturally when Pharaoh heard that all the baby boys were still alive he questioned Shiphrah and Puah as to why they had not done as he had ordered. Not only were these women brave but they were clever too, and gave Pharaoh a perfectly reasonable answer. They told him that because the Hebrew women were so healthy their babies were born before they, the midwives, arrived.

God remembered these two brave women, Shiphrah and Puah. He gave them families of their own because they believed in him. God still wants us to believe in him today. Other people may laugh at us or even be unkind to us because we believe in God but he knows if we are trusting in him. He wants us to listen to what he says in the Bible and not to disobey his commands. One of these commands is to love God. Shiphrah and Puah loved God enough to know that what Pharaoh wanted them to do was wrong. Do you love God enough to risk facing the anger of others rather than go against his laws?

Pharaoh however was still determined to do something to stop the Hebrews from becoming even more numerous. He ordered that every Hebrew baby boy was to be thrown into the river Nile. Only the baby girls were to be allowed to live.

This was the situation into which the baby Moses was born. His parents were from the family of Levi, one of the twelve tribes of the Hebrew people. Moses was a strong, healthy child and his mother was so afraid for his life that she hid him for three months. But she realised that sooner or later her little son would be found so she thought of a plan.

Moses' mother made a little basket of reeds and coated it with tar to keep out the water. Then she placed her son in the basket and hid it in the reeds growing by the banks of the river Nile. We can only imagine how sad she must have been to leave her child on his own and yet she knew that if she kept Moses any longer his life would be in real danger.

Moses' elder sister watched from a distance and waited to see what would happen to her baby brother. First to appear at the river were Pharaoh's daughter and her servants. The Egyptian princess had come down to the river to bathe. When she saw the basket she sent one of her servants to get it. Inside the basket was the baby Moses and like most babies taken away from their mothers he was crying. Pharaoh's daughter felt very sorry for the little boy although she knew that he was a Hebrew child and that her father wanted all such baby boys to be killed. But she was not a cruel person like her father.

Meanwhile Moses' sister had seen what had happened and approached the princess. She asked her if she would go and get a Hebrew woman to look after the baby. Pharaoh's daughter agreed and Moses' sister came back with her mother. So Moses was returned to his own mother who was to look after him for the Egyptian princess. How pleased she must have been to have her little boy back. Moses' mother must have wondered if she would ever see her son again when she hid him away beside the river Nile. Now she would be able to care for him again without fearing for his life.

We can see even at this early stage in Moses' life that God was watching over him and caring for him. God cares for us all, whether we are old or young but we must trust him and believe in what he tells us in his Word, the Bible. God has given the Bible to help us in our lives and to tell us about himself. We should read our Bibles as much as we

And when she opened it, she saw the child . . . (Exodus 2, v.6).

can and get to know them well.

When Moses was a little older his mother took him to Pharaoh's daughter and Moses became her son. In fact it is only now that Moses is given his name. The princess called him Moses because she had taken him from the water. The name Moses sounds like the Hebrew for draw out.

We know nothing of what kind of childhood Moses had as the Bible moves from the point when he is given back to Pharaoh's daughter to the time that Moses had become an adult. However we can guess what kind of life Moses led. From being in danger of losing his life he had become as one of Pharaoh's grandchildren. He must have enjoyed great luxury and many privileges as the son of Pharaoh's daughter. He would have lived in a splendid palace and been free from the hardships that his own people, the Hebrews, had to suffer.

How different his life would have been had he remained with his own people. But God, in order to keep Moses from danger, placed him in the safest household in Egypt, that of Pharaoh. God always knows what is best for us and we should remember this even when we have problems and worries. So often we wonder why things happen but we cannot see as God sees. We do not know what could happen in the next hour, or even the next minute, but God knows what will happen to us throughout our whole lives.

One day Moses went to see where his people lived. There he saw how the Hebrews suffered as they worked under the harsh rule of the Egyptians. An Egyptian was beating one of the Hebrews and Moses was so angered by this that he killed the man. To murder anyone is very wrong no matter what the situation and Moses did not just act in a fit of temper. First he looked around to see if anyone was watching and then he killed the Egyptian. Next he hid the body in the sand.

However Moses' action had not gone un-noticed. The very next day he came upon two Hebrews fighting each other. Moses tried to stop them but one of the men said to him; 'Who made you a judge over us? Are you going to kill me like you killed the Egyptian yesterday.' Moses was very afraid and realised that his crime was known.

Pharaoh too had learned of Moses' action and tried to kill him. But Moses ran away from Egypt and went to the land of Midian. Even though Moses had done a terrible wrong God was still looking after him and protecting him from danger. God deals with us in the same way. We have all done wrong. We surely won't have killed anyone but we know that we often do things that are wrong and yet God does not forget us. In fact he loves us so much that he sent his son Jesus to die for our sins so that we can be accepted by God. Just as Moses had much for which to thank God we too will always be in God's debt.

After his journey from Egypt Moses must have been very tired so he stopped at a well to get a drink of water and to rest himself. While he was there Moses saw seven girls with some sheep which belonged to their father. They had come to get water for themselves and the sheep. But as they tried to get water the girls were driven away by other shepherds. When Moses saw the way they were being treated he helped them. The girls returned home leaving Moses by the well. He must have been wondering what he was going to do next. If he went back to Egypt he would be in danger of losing his life if Pharaoh found out that he had returned. Moses may even have wondered if his own people would accept him back. After all, he had been brought up as an Egyptian prince not a Hebrew slave. Moses need not have worried because as we shall see God had a purpose for him even in the foreign land of Midian.

Sometimes things happen to us that we do not really understand and perhaps even frighten us. But if we are trusting in God we should not be afraid. We must remember that he will care for us whatever our situation in life.

But Moses stood up and helped them, and watered their flock. (Exodus 2, v.17).

CHAPTER 2

Refuge in Midian

Moses did not have to wonder what to do with himself for very long. When the girls he had helped got home their father Reuel asked them why they had come back so soon. They told him of how Moses had helped them and so Reuel insisted that Moses be brought into their home to have a meal with him and his family.

Reuel was very kind to Moses and so he agreed to stay with Reuel and his family. In fact Moses must have been extremely popular with Reuel because he allowed his daughter Zipporah to marry Moses. Zipporah had a baby boy whom Moses named Gershom. Yet despite all the kindness shown to him Moses knew that these people who had taken him in and treated him as a member of their family were not his own people.

While Moses had settled, at least for the time being, the Hebrews in Egypt were still suffering greatly at the hands of their cruel masters. Even though the king who had been ruling at the time when Moses fled had died, the Hebrew people were no better off. They must have felt that God had forgotten them but he had not. He heard their cries and because the Hebrews were his special people God began to work in a way that would help his people. Moses was to play a large part in the events that followed.

God is in control of our lives and we must never think that he has forgotten us. Nor should we imagine that we can forget about him. Some people are only interested in God as a way to get what they want or as someone to turn to when they have problems. We must remember God at all times; not only when we have difficulties but also when things are going well for us. There is always so much for

Call him, that he may eat bread. And Moses was content to dwell with the man . . . (Exodus 2, vs.20,21).

which we should be thankful to God.

So while the Hebrew people suffered in Egypt Moses continued to work for his father-in-law, Reuel. One day Moses was looking after some sheep belonging to Reuel and he led them to a mountain called Horeb. There he saw an amazing sight. In front of him was a bush on fire yet despite the flames the bush was not burning up. Wondering what kind of strange bush this could be Moses went over to look.

As you may have guessed God had planned this event and was watching Moses when he came over to the bush. Then God spoke to Moses from the bush. He told Moses to take off his sandals because he was standing on holy ground. That may sound a bit odd to us but in eastern countries to take off your shoes before entering a holy place was seen as a sign of respect. Then God explained to Moses who he was. 'I am the God of your father, the God of Abraham, the God of Isaac, and the God of Jacob.' Moses was so terrified by what he heard that he hid his face. He was afraid to look at God.

But God carried on speaking and told Moses that he was to go back to Egypt and to lead the Hebrews out of the country. Moses was so astonished at the idea of him leading his people out of Egypt that he began to make excuses. How like us. We are always making excuses for not doing things but we must be ready to do what God wants us to do. If we trust him he will help us no matter how hard the task may seem.

First of all, Moses said, 'I'm not important enough to go to Pharaoh and take all the Hebrew people out of Egypt.' But God promised Moses that he would help him and told him again that he was to lead the Hebrews out of Egypt to worship God on Mount Horeb.

Moses' next excuse was to ask who he should tell the Hebrews had sent him. So God told Moses what to say and explained to him what he was to do. Moses was to tell the

And he looked, and behold, the bush burned with fire, and the bush was not consumed. (Exodus 3, v.2).

Hebrews that God had promised to bring them into another land where they would be free from the slavery of Egypt. God always keeps his promises and works everything out in his own time which is the best time.

Then God showed Moses his power by telling him exactly how the king of Egypt would react when he was asked to let the Hebrew nation go. The king would refuse and God would cause miraculous events to happen. Finally the king would let the Hebrews go and when they left they would be given all kinds of goods by the Egyptians.

Despite having been told all this Moses was still afraid to go. 'What if they do not believe me and say that God never spoke to me?' Once again God showed his power to Moses. He turned Moses' staff into a snake and then told Moses to pick up the snake by its tail. Moses trusted God enough to do as he was told although he must have been worried about the snake. But amazingly when he took hold of the snake it turned back into a staff. '"This," said the Lord, "is so that they may believe that the Lord, the God of their fathers — the God of Abraham, the God of Isaac, and the God of Jacob — has appeared to you."'

Before Moses could say anything he was given another demonstration of God's power. He was told to put his hand into his cloak and when he took it out his hand was covered with leprosy, a very unpleasant disease. God then told Moses to replace his hand in his cloak and this time when he brought it out there was no sign of leprosy.

As a final display of power if no-one believed these signs Moses was to pour some water from the Nile onto dry ground and the water would turn to blood.

Yet Moses himself was still doubtful and he began to make further excuses. He said that he would be unable to speak in front of people as he would have to. But God reminded him that he would help him to speak.

At last Moses admitted what he had been feeling all along. He just did not want to go. 'O Lord, please send someone else to do it.'

God became angry with Moses. He said that his brother Aaron would speak for him while he would still help them both to do as he wished. God would help them not only in their speaking but also in all their actions as well.

Although Moses was a very special servant of God there is much that we can learn from these amazing happenings. They show us not only God's tremendous power but also his great patience. Despite being shown these signs of God's power Moses was reluctant to believe that the God who had done these miracles could help him if he went back to Egypt. He did not realise that if God was on his side he need have no fear of what would happen to him.

If we are trusting in God we too need not be afraid of what lies ahead. God has everything planned for the best. But we must not question the way that he does things. He is the one who has made us so what right have we to complain or think we know best?

God was not pleased with Moses because of his unbelief but he did not abandon him and get someone else to take on the work that Moses was so keen to avoid. God could easily have done so but he had chosen Moses for this task. Sometimes we try to get out of doing things that we do not want to do but if we ask God to help us even those very hard things can be done. We must never refuse to do something that God wants us to do.

If we were faced with someone like Moses who was always making excuses for not getting on with his task how would we react? Surely our patience would have been exhausted and we would have gone to find somebody else to do the work. We would probably have been very angry at his unbelief.

God would have every right to reject us because we do not believe as we ought yet he has not dealt with us as we deserve. Should we not ask God to forgive us for our unbelief? Can we not see that God has been so patient with

us? He has given us many good things in life and yet we
hardly remember to thank him. We know that we should
thank those who give us gifts so how much more ought we
to be thankful to God. His greatest gift is his son Jesus who
was sent to save us from the punishment that we deserved
for our wrongdoing. Jesus took our punishment so that
God would accept us. It does not please God to reject
anyone but if we will not have Jesus as our Saviour he will
make us take our punishment for ourselves. How thankful
we should be that God has given us Jesus to be our Saviour
and that through him we can become the children of God.

God's final words to Moses were to take his staff with
him to Egypt so that he could perform miracles with it.
God did not need to use anything to help Moses to do this
but perhaps the staff would remind him of what God had
already shown him. Surely every time Moses saw the staff
he would remember it being turned into a snake and then
back to a staff.

Moses now realised that the time for making excuses
was past. He had to do as God said and go back to Egypt to
rescue his own people, the Hebrews. Moses had been
chosen by God for this purpose and there was no point in
delaying any longer.

Moses had been given a great work to do and in
preparation for it God had allowed Moses to come into his
very presence. There had been no priest with Moses when
God spoke to him from the burning bush. No-one else had
come to Moses saying that God had sent them to tell him
what he was to do. God himself had given Moses the
details of the work to be done in Egypt. What a great
privilege Moses was given.

God has given us many privileges too. He has provided
us with the Bible to help us in our lives. He has provided
us with food and clothing and so many other good things.
We must ask God to help us to be truly thankful to him.
Above all we should be thankful to God for his love to us.

God gave his son, Jesus, so that those who believe in him will go to heaven and be with God for ever. What a wonderful God we have. Trust in him as your heavenly father and ask him to help you to believe in Jesus.

CHAPTER 3

Back to Egypt

After his meeting with God Moses returned to his father-in-law and asked to be allowed to go back to Egypt to see if any of his own people, the Hebrews, were still alive. Reuel, or Jethro as he was also known, must have felt sorry that his son-in-law wanted to leave and return to Egypt. However he did not try to stop him from going. Perhaps he thought he understood Moses' wish to see his own people again. All that Jethro said was, 'Go, and I wish you well.'

So Moses set off with his wife and sons. He also took 'the staff of God in his hand'. This was the staff which God had used to show Moses his power. With it Moses was going to show the Egyptians how great his God was.

While Moses was on his way back to Egypt God told Aaron, Moses' brother, to go out into the desert to meet him. They must have been delighted to see each other after such a long time. It had been many years since Moses had fled from Egypt. Moses told Aaron all that God had said to him and about the miraculous signs that he was to perform. Then they returned to Egypt.

All the leaders of the tribes and families of the Hebrews were asked to a meeting by Moses and Aaron. As God had said, Aaron spoke to the people and told them all that had been said to Moses. Then the leaders were shown the miracles that God had performed before Moses. The people believed what they had been told and realising that God indeed cared for them, they began to worship him. Just as God had foretold the people had believed and accepted Moses and Aaron as their leaders.

Moses and Aaron then went to Pharoah and said to him,

And Moses took his wife and sons, and set them upon an ass, and he returned to the land of Egypt . . . (Exodus 4, v.20).

And Moses and Aaron went and gathered together all the elders of the children of Israel . . . (Exodus 4, v.29).

'This is what the Lord, the God of Israel says, "Let my people go, so that they may worship me in the desert."' But Pharaoh did not acknowledge the God of Israel and refused to let the Hebrews go. Then Moses and Aaron identified the Lord as the God of the Hebrews. This time Pharaoh knew who they were talking about but he was only angry that the Hebrews were being kept from their hard labour.

Today many people are like Pharaoh. They say, 'Who is God that I ought to worship him? I am in control of my own life.' Sadly they are making the biggest mistake of their lives. One day we will all stand before God and he will deal with us as we deserve. Those who have given no thought to God, he will reject but those who have accepted his son, Jesus, as Saviour he will welcome. You can ask Jesus to be your Saviour now for he has said, 'Him that cometh unto me, I will in no wise cast out.'

In fact Pharaoh was sure that the reason why the Hebrews wanted to worship God was due to them being lazy. So he thought of a plan which would force the Hebrews to work even harder. He told the foremen who were in charge of the Hebrews not to supply them with any straw to make bricks. They were to say that they would have to get their own straw. But even with all this extra work the same numbers of bricks had to be made. Pharaoh felt confident that this would put an end to Moses' pleas to let them go away to worship God.

Of course the poor Hebrews had an impossible task and when they did not make as many bricks as before some of the leaders were beaten by the Egyptians. They complained to Pharaoh but he was as angry as ever and sent them back to work. Moses and Aaron were waiting to meet the men after they had seen Pharaoh but they did not get much of a welcome. 'What good have you done? See how much Pharaoh hates our people now.' The leaders blamed Moses and Aaron for all their troubles.

Moses and Aaron went in, and told Pharaoh . . . (Exodus 5, v.1).

Although Moses had been told by God that Pharaoh would refuse to let the Hebrews go he now began to question God. Why had this happened? Not only had Pharaoh refused to let them go he had made life almost impossible for the Hebrews. Aren't we like this? When things go wrong or not in the way we would like we are so quick to doubt the wisdom of God's actions. Yet he has told us in the Bible that if we love him and trust in him all things will work together for our good.

Despite Moses' worries God had a purpose in all these events. He intended to show both the Hebrews and the Egyptians how great a God he was. By God's power Pharaoh would be forced to let the Hebrews go. God told Moses that he had made a covenant or agreement with the people of Israel and that they had a special place in God's eyes.

Moses related all this to the Israelites but they would not listen to him. They would not believe that they were God's chosen people. They felt that things were even worse for them than ever before so how could they be special to God? But God did not show any anger and told Moses to go back to Pharaoh and ask again that he let the Israelites leave Egypt.

As we saw earlier Moses was eager to find some excuse. This time it was one that he had used before. He protested that he could not speak in public. To support his excuse Moses pointed out that if his own people would not listen to him, surely Pharaoh would be even less likely to do so. But God again told Moses that Aaron would speak for him. By his actions Moses would show Pharaoh the power of the true God.

So Moses and Aaron obeyed God and returned to Pharaoh. To show God's power Aaron threw down his staff and it turned into a snake. But then Pharaoh's magicians turned their staffs into snakes. Amazingly Aaron's snake swallowed up those belonging to the magi-

cians. Yet Pharaoh still refused to listen to Moses and
Aaron who then left him.

It would be a mistake for us to think that this struggle
was between Moses and Pharaoh because it wasn't. God
was using his servant Moses to demonstrate his power. In
fact God was about to show Pharaoh and all the Egyptians
some examples of his great power. He did this by sending
ten plagues on Egypt. The real struggle was between the
power of God and the evil power of Satan.

First there was the plague of blood. In Pharaoh's presence Moses struck the water of the river Nile and it
turned to blood. All the fish died and the river stank so
much that the Egyptians had to do without water until
they dug for it in other places. But Pharaoh's magicians
also turned water to blood so Pharaoh stubbornly refused
to let the Hebrews go and took very little notice of this
awful plague. Certainly as king of Egypt his servants
would have made sure that he got clean water so as long as
he was not suffering he did not care about others.

Seven days later God sent Moses back again to Pharaoh
to tell him that if he did not let the Israelites go, a plague of
frogs would come on the whole country. So the whole of
Egypt was filled with frogs and although the magicians
made frogs appear they could not make them go away.
Pharaoh sent for Moses and Aaron to ask them to pray to
God to take away the frogs. Moses told Pharaoh to set a
time for the plague of frogs to end so that he would know
that God alone had been able to get rid of them. Pharaoh
chose the next day. Perhaps he hoped that the frogs would
have disappeared by then but they did not. God caused all
the frogs to die the next day but Pharaoh still refused to let
the Hebrews leave the country.

The next plague came without warning, a plague of
gnats or lice followed by a plague of flies. The flies ruined
the land of Egypt but in the land of Goshen, where the
Israelites lived, there were no flies at all. Again Pharaoh

And the frogs came up, and covered the land of Egypt. (Exodus 8, v.6).

promised to let them go if the flies were taken away but when God did so Pharaoh changed his mind.

The next plague came on the animals kept by the Egyptians: the horses, donkeys, camels, cattle, sheep, and goats. While the animals belonging to the Israelites were unharmed those belonging to the Egyptians died. But Pharaoh still would not obey God and so a plague of boils broke out on all the Egyptian people. The magicians were so ill that they could not even stand before Moses and Aaron.

The seventh plague was a tremendous hailstorm. God said that it would be so strong that any person or animal who was not under shelter when the hail came would be killed. It happened just as God said it would and Pharaoh begged Moses to ask God to end the plague. God did as Moses asked, the storm ended, but Pharaoh still would not let the Hebrews go.

So God sent a plague of locusts which ate up any plants and crops that had not already been destroyed. Once again Pharaoh pleaded for the plague to end but his stubbornness continued. Darkness then fell on Egypt, a darkness that could be felt. This was no natural event because as with the other plagues it did not affect the Israelites at all.

One last plague was to fall upon the Egyptians and it was the most terrible of all. In every family in Egypt the eldest child would die and even the animals were to be affected.

Before this last terrible plague came God told Moses and Aaron about a special meal that the Israelites were to take. Every member of every family was to eat this meal. The Israelites were to take a lamb and roast it and then eat it. Any part that was not eaten was to be burnt. The blood from the lamb was to be sprinkled on the doorposts. When God would come to carry out the last plague he would see the blood on the doorposts and pass over that house. All the people were to be ready to leave immediately.

The meal was to be called the Passover and would have a

And they shall take of the blood and strike it on the two side posts and on the upper door post . . . and when I see the blood, I will pass over you, when I smite the land of Egypt. (Exodus 12, vs.7,13).

very important place in the worship of the Israelites.
When they ate the meal they would remember the power
of God and the miraculous way in which he had brought
his people out of Egypt. They would remember the special
details that God commanded them to follow. If their
children asked them what the Passover meant they would
tell them how God passed over the houses of the Israelites
and struck down the Egyptians.

Maybe it seems a strange thing to do, to have sprinkled
blood on the doorposts. God didn't need the blood as a
sign because he knew who his people were but the blood is
a sign for us today. Just as the blood of the lamb saved the
Israelites from death so the blood of Jesus, God's son,
saves us from sin. Jesus is often spoken of as the lamb of
God in the Bible. Many parts of the Old Testament that
speak about the rules for the Israelites to worship God and
of their need to be forgiven for their sins represent the way
in which we too need to be forgiven for our sins by
believing that Jesus died and rose again to save us, that his
blood cleans up the horrible thing in our lives that is sin.

At midnight the final plague came on the Egyptians.
Pharaoh realised at last that he could not oppose God so in
the middle of the night he sent for Moses and Aaron. He
told them to leave immediately with all the tribes and
families of Israel, and all their flocks and herds. The effect
of the plague had been so great that every family in Egypt
lost at least one person. At last the Israelites were free to go
and worship the true God.

As we shall see although Pharaoh had finally let the
Israelites go it was not because he trusted in God. God's
power had forced him to give in but there was still unbelief
in his heart. Pharaoh had brought great sadness on his
people and destruction in his land because of his stubborn
unbelief.

Unbelief will bring sadness in our own lives. God wants
us to believe and trust in him but if we do not we will be

punished. But if we trust in God's son, Jesus, God will not punish us. He has already punished Jesus for our sins. If we believe in Jesus, God will look on us as his children. He will treat us far better than our earthly fathers for he knows us better than even our parents. The Bible tells us that God is so good that he is more willing to give than we are to receive. Surely we can see from this how much God loves us and cares for us.

CHAPTER 4

The Exodus

Not only was Pharaoh glad to see the back of the Israelites but all the Egyptians urged the people to leave as well. They were afraid that they would all die if the Israelites stayed a moment longer. Moses had told the people to ask the Egyptians for gold and silver and clothing and when they did the Egyptians were only too willing to give up their possessions. This was exactly what God had said would happen. When he had spoken to Moses on Mount Horeb he foretold that when the Israelites left Egypt they would take away much of the goods of the Egyptians. So at last the Israelites set out from Egypt, a huge crowd of people with all their sheep and cattle as well.

600,000 men as well as all the women and children left Egypt. Today this would be like the whole of a big city marching out of their homes. The Israelites had been living in Egypt for 430 years since the time of Joseph. But now at God's command they were setting out on a great journey.

We are all involved in a journey, that is the journey of life. We don't know where life will lead us but God does and he wants us to give our lives to him and he will guide us on our journey. Then as we reach the end of the road and leave this world God will take us to heaven to be with him for ever.

The great mass of the Israelites left Rameses in Egypt and travelled to a place called Succoth. They were led by God towards the Red Sea. After the Israelites had left Succoth they camped at a place called Etham which was at the edge of the desert.

Nowadays we have maps and signs to help us to find our

And the Lord went before them by day in a pillar of cloud . . .
(Exodus 13, v.21).

way on a journey but the Israelites had no such aids. How
were they going to get to their destination? How was God
going to lead them?

God made things very easy for the people and gave them
all the guidance they needed. God himself was with his
people all the time, by day in a pillar of cloud and by night
in a pillar of fire. This meant that the Israelites could travel
just as easily at night because of the light that came from
the fire.

God is still with those who love him and he continues to
guide them as clearly as in the past. We may not have such
obvious helps as pillars of cloud and fire but our greatest
guide is the Bible. If we follow its teaching we will be on
the right path. We also have the tremendous privilege of
being able to pray to God at any time. God has promised to
hear and answer our prayers. What a thought this is, that
weak and sinful as we are God listens to our prayers.
Prayer and Bible study are very necessary parts of the
Christian life but we must remember that they will not be
of any value to us if we have not accepted Jesus Christ as
our Saviour.

Some people say, 'I read my Bible, and I pray, but it just
doesn't help me at all.' They seem to forget that we cannot
be accepted by God because of our own efforts, we must
trust in Jesus alone. The Bible tells us that Jesus says 'I am
the way, the truth, and the life, no man comes to the
Father but by me.' Only by relying on Jesus will we be
walking on the right road.

As the Israelites journeyed on, led by God, he spoke
again to Moses. He told Moses to tell the Israelites to turn
back and camp near a place called Pi Hahiroth, between
Migdol and the sea. God had a plan that would show both
the Israelites and the Egyptians how great a God he was.

God said to Moses that Pharaoh would think the
Israelites were lost and wandering around the land and
would come after them with his army. So the Israelites did

as God said and camped at Pi Hahiroth.

Just as God predicted Pharaoh was regretting his decision to let the Israelites go and came after them with a great army. As he and his men approached the camp all the Israelites were terrified and turned on Moses. Had he brought them out just to die in the desert? Why hadn't he left them alone to serve the Egyptians? Here they were, trapped. The Red Sea was in front of them, the Egyptian army behind. No wonder they were so afraid!

But Moses told the people not to be afraid as God would defeat the Egyptians and save them. 'The Egyptians you see today you will never see again.' God then said to Moses, 'Raise your staff and stretch out your hand over the sea to divide the water so that the Israelites can go through the sea on dry ground.'

Moses did as God had told him and all that night God caused a strong east wind to blow and the sea was driven back. The Israelites were then able to continue their journey on dry land with a wall of water on their right and on their left.

Perhaps you are wondering what on earth had happened to Pharaoh and his army. If he was so close that the Israelites had seen him and his men why had he not attacked the helpless Israelites? During that whole long night why had Pharoah not come any closer?

The answer lay in the way that God had protected his special people. The pillar of cloud had come to rest between the Israelites and the advancing Egyptian army. So for the whole night the distance between the two camps remained the same. Not only did the cloud prevent the Egyptians from getting any nearer the Israelites, it brought them darkness yet it gave light to the Hebrews.

But when Pharaoh and his army saw the Israelites crossing the Red Sea they chased after them and followed them into what had been the sea. However God was still watching over his people and he made the wheels of the

And the children of Israel went into the midst of the sea upon the dry ground . . . (Exodus 14, v.22).

Egyptian chariots swerve so that the drivers had difficulty in controlling them. In fact they were so afraid that the Egyptians cried out, 'Let's get away from the Israelites. The Lord is fighting for them against Egypt.'

Then God told Moses to stretch out his hand over the sea again so that the water would return to its usual place, trapping the Egyptian army. Moses did as God commanded him and at dawn the seas surged back to their place and the fleeing Egyptians were drowned. Not one of them survived.

But God's chosen people, the Israelites, travelled on unharmed. When they saw the miraculous way in which God had saved them, 'the people feared the Lord and put their trust in him and in Moses his servant.'

God wants us to put our trust in him now just as his people did. We should also learn to fear God, not in the way we are usually afraid but by realising God's great power, and understanding that he is in control of this world. Only by obeying God in what he has told us in his Word, the Bible, will we be able to live lives that please him.

We are also told that the Israelites put their trust in Moses, God's servant. We too, should be ready to take advice from those whom God has chosen to teach us. We ought to listen to what older Christians have to say because we can learn a lot from them. By taking their advice we may avoid some difficulty that they themselves fell into. So often we think we know best but God may use others to show us our mistakes.

Moses and the Israelites were so thankful to God for saving them from the Egyptians that they sang a song of praise to God. In the song they told of the wonderful way in which God had protected them. They realised how great God was and knew that without his help they would still have been slaves in Egypt.

From the Red Sea Moses led the Israelites into the

Desert of Shur. For three days they travelled through the desert and found no water. When they finally found water at Marah they could not drink it because it was bad. The people began to complain and as before they turned on Moses. 'What are we going to drink?', they said.

Once again God helped his people by performing a miracle. Moses cried out to God who showed him a piece of wood. When Moses threw the piece of wood into the water it no longer tasted bad. So God provided water for his people.

God also gave the Israelites a promise that if they followed his commands and obeyed his laws none of the things that happened to the Egyptians would come upon them. This was a wonderful promise but sadly the people of Israel did not always keep God's laws.

The Israelites travelled from Marah to Elim where there was plenty water; twelve springs and seventy palm trees. There they camped before setting out once more to reach the desert of Sin, between Elim and Sinai. Once again the people began to grumble against Moses and Aaron. 'If only you had left us alone in Egypt where we had as much food as we wanted. You have only led us out here to starve us to death.'

It certainly had not taken the Israelites very long to forget God's power or his care for them. Surely they did not think that God was just going to leave them to die in the desert. Whatever they did think God again came to their rescue by performing another miracle.

God told Moses that he would provide food for the people who were to go out each day and gather just enough for that one day except on the sixth day when they would gather enough food to last for two days. God intended to test the people to see if they would follow his instructions.

So Moses and Aaron spoke to all the Israelites telling them that God had heard their grumbling. The people were also reminded that it wasn't Moses and Aaron they

were grumbling against but God himself. As the whole
Israelite people looked towards the desert they saw the
cloud again and knew that God was present.

In the morning there was a layer of dew on the ground.
When the dew had gone, thin frost-like flakes appeared.
The Israelites were puzzled and asked themselves what it
was, so Moses told them. 'It is the bread the Lord has
given you to eat.' So the people gathered their food. Some
gathered a lot while others gathered only a little but when
they measured it those who had gathered a lot did not have
too much and those who gathered a little did not have too
little. Moses told the Israelites not to keep any until the
morning.

However some people paid no attention to what Moses
had said and kept some of the food until the next morning.
But it was full of maggots and began to smell. Naturally
Moses was angry with these people for disobeying God's
command. On the sixth day the people collected twice as
much and on the next day there were no maggots and the
food did not stink. Perhaps you are wondering why the
people were not to gather food on the seventh day. This
was because it was a holy day, a day of rest, the Sabbath.
God made the world in six days and on the seventh day he
rested and made it a holy day. This is still one of God's
laws and we should remember to keep the Sabbath day,
Sunday, properly. On that day we should go to church to
hear God's word being explained and try to spend as much
time as possible in reading our Bibles and praying to God.
We must try to keep it a holy day. People think that it is
silly to keep a command which was given thousands of
years ago but they forget that God never changes. His laws
were not meant just for the Israelites but for all people at
all times.

Sadly even as today many people do not keep God's holy
day there were Israelites too who disobeyed God's law.
They went out on the seventh day to gather food but they

were unable to find any. But God was angry. 'How long will you refuse to keep my commands and my instructions?' he said to Moses.

The Israelites called the food manna, which actually means 'what is it?' For forty years the people were given manna until they reached the border of Canaan. God commanded Moses to put some manna in a jar and keep it so that their descendants would remember the way that God had provided food for his people.

From the desert of Sin all the Israelite people moved on, travelling from place to place as God commanded them. They camped at Rephidim but there was no water for the people to drink. As before they quarrelled with Moses and demanded that he give them water to drink.

Again Moses had to remind the people that they were angering God by their constant grumbling. But the Israelites went on complaining. 'Why did you bring us out of Egypt to make us die of thirst?' Moses cried out to God afraid that the people might even stone him. Once again God came to the help of his faithful servant Moses and his less faithful people, the Israelites.

He told Moses to walk on ahead of the people taking with him some of the leaders and also his staff. At Horeb he was to strike a rock with the staff and water would come out of it. Moses did as he was commanded and the people got their water. Moses called the place Massah, which means testing; and Meribah, which means quarrelling. There the Israelites had quarrelled and tested God.

As we have seen God was very patient with the Israelites despite their forgetfulness of his care for them. We must make sure that we do not forget about God or his goodness to us. He is just as patient with us and if we are really honest we will have to admit that at times we are no better than the Israelites of old. We must try to serve God in everything that we do. God will help us if we trust in him and our lives will be so much better.

Thou shalt smite the rock, and there shall come water out of it . . . And Moses did so in the sight of the elders of Israel. (Exodux 17, v.6).

After their grumblings about food and water the Israelites soon had something else to worry them. Another tribe, the Amalekites, attacked the Israelites at Rephidim. But Moses said to Joshua, 'Choose some men and go out and fight the Amalekites.' So the next day Joshua went out with his chosen men and fought the Amalekites. As the two armies fought, Moses, Aaron, and Hur, another leader, watched from the top of a hill. As long as Moses held up his hands the Israelites were winning the battle but when he lowered them then the Amalekites began to win. So when Moses' hands grew tired, they sat him on a stone and Aaron and Hur held up his hands. The battle raged on but at last Joshua and his men defeated the Amalekites.

Then God told Moses to write down on a scroll all that happened, because God planned to destoy the Amalekites. They would not believe that it was God who worked miracles for the Israelites and they had also attacked God's chosen people.

News of all these miraculous events and happenings that God had brought about to help Moses and the Israelites had reached Jethro, Moses' father-in-law.

While Moses had been leading his people out of Egypt Jethro had looked after Moses' wife Zipporah and his two sons, Gershom and Eliezer. But now Jethro sent word to Moses saying he was coming to meet him with his wife and sons.

So Moses went out to meet Jethro. He must have been very happy to see his wife and sons again as well as his father-in-law. We can only guess at how long it was since Moses had seen his family but it must have been quite a lengthy period if the Israelites had to walk everywhere. With so many people and children too they would not have been able to go very fast.

After Moses and Jethro had greeted each other they went into one of the tents. There Moses told his father-in-

Aaron and Hur stayed up his hands, the one on the one side, and the other on the other side . . . (Exodus 17, v.12).

law about all that had happened since he had left him; of how God had looked after them and saved them from Pharaoh and the Egyptians and helped them during their travels.

Jethro was so pleased about all the good things that God had done for the Israelites that he began to praise God. 'Now I know that the Lord is greater than all other gods.' Then he made an offering to God, and Aaron and the other Israelite leaders ate a meal with Jethro.

We should always be ready to praise God for he has given us so many things. Neither should we be boastful about anything we do because it is God's right to receive any praise or glory. When Moses told Jethro about what had happened he didn't say 'I did this' or 'I did that' and take the credit himself. Instead he gave God the glory and praise for keeping the Hebrew nation safe.

The next day Moses spent all his time making decisions about any disagreements that had arisen between the people. From morning till night he carried out the job of a judge in a court making his decisions in agreement with God's laws and commands.

Jethro saw all this and gave Moses some very good advice. 'The work is too heavy for you; you cannot handle it alone.' Then he told Moses to choose certain good men and make them officials over thousands, hundreds, fifties and tens. They could then serve as judges for the people and only if they had a very hard case to deal with would they come to Moses. Everyone would be better pleased. The people would not have to wait to see Moses and he would have a lot less work to do. Remember that when they left Egypt there were 600,000 men as well as women and children. So Moses was the leader of a number of people who would today fill up quite a big city. You can imagine how hard his task was. In fact if God had not helped Moses he just could not have managed.

Wisely, Moses took the good advice of Jethro and chose

men to act as judges leaving him to deal with only the most difficult cases. After this Jethro went back to his own country having helped Moses greatly in his difficult task as the leader of the Israelites.

We should always be prepared to listen to good advice just like Moses. He could have ignored what Jethro said. After all wasn't he a very important person? God had made him leader of a great company of people so why should he listen to Jethro? But Moses didn't think like that at all. He was not too proud to accept the advice that Jethro gave him. It would be good for us to remember this event anytime we are given good advice. Are we going to accept it humbly and be thankful for the wisdom of someone else or are we going to be obstinate and imagine that we know best and ignore the advice?

CHAPTER 5

At Mount Sinai

It was now three months since the children of Israel had left Egypt and they had reached the desert of Sinai in front of the mountain which was also called Sinai. Here the Israelites set up their camp. It must have been an enormous camp with over 600,000 men and all the women and children, and the cattle and other animals.

Then Moses climbed up Mount Sinai and there God spoke to Moses. He reminded Moses of how he had destroyed the Egyptians and how he had cared for and protected the Israelites. Then God said that if Moses and the Israelites kept his commands and obeyed him at all times 'then out of all nations you will be my treasured possession.' What a wonderful promise!

After hearing this great promise Moses went back down the mountain and called together all the leaders and told them exactly what God had said. They agreed that they would do as God had commanded so Moses returned to the mountain with the people's answer.

God then told Moses to get all the people to carry out certain instructions so that they would be ready for the third day. On that day God would come down on Mount Sinai in a thick cloud in view of all his people. The people would see the majesty of God and would realise that the laws which Moses would give them had been spoken to him by God himself.

The reason why the people had to prepare themselves was that God being holy could not appear directly before the Israelites. Not that his power was limited but that the people would be unable to look on God in his complete majesty and holiness. Prepared as they were the people

And there Israel camped before the mount. (Exodus 19, v.2).

would only see the thick cloud which covered God's glory.

Mount Sinai itself was to be shut off from the people. Anyone who touched even the foot of the mountain was to be put to death. Only when there was a loud trumpet sound were the people to be allowed up on the mountain.

On the morning of the third day there was thunder and lightning and a thick cloud covered the mountain. A very loud trumpet blast could be heard. Everyone in the camp was trembling. But Moses led the people out of the camp to meet God and they all stood at the foot of Mount Sinai, just as they had been commanded to do. The mountain was covered with smoke because God had come down in fire. The sound of the trumpet grew louder and louder.

God called Moses to the top of the mountain and immediately sent him down again to warn the people not to try to come onto the mountain. Moses' reply was to suggest that as God has already given commands forbidding the Israelites to go up on Mount Sinai he didn't need to remind them again. But God knew that the people would want to know what was happening and that the priests who might have felt more holy than the ordinary people would try to come onto the mountain.

So Moses returned to the Israelites again having been instructed to bring only Aaron with him and told the people all that God had said to him.

Why were all the people not allowed on the mountain? Why did they have to prepare themselves for two whole days? Perhaps all these instructions seem unnecessary. But we must remember that God himself, the creator of everything in the universe, was going to appear on Mount Sinai. It was a very special event and the people had to realise the greatness of God and the wonder of what was happening before them. God was going to speak to Moses and give him the laws by which the Israelites were to be governed.

God is a holy God and cannot look on sin. He is a just

God and must punish sin. But he is a merciful God and has punished his son Jesus for our sins so that we can come before him. We are not kept apart from God. We can speak to him at any time. What we must do is to trust in Jesus and give our lives to him. Only then will we be able to live as God would have us to live.

The most important of the laws that God gave to Moses are those known as the Ten Commandments. These laws were not just for the Israelites at that time but for all people for all time. God still requires us to keep the commandments but we must remember that we will never be able to keep them perfectly and so we must trust in Jesus, the one who never sinned in any way.

The first four commandments tell us our duty to God, and the remaining six tell us about our duty to other people. These laws were given by God so that people who lived by them would be blessed. We are told how to worship God and reminded that he is the only true God. We are also taught to respect other people's lives, property and all their belongings.

All God's laws are for our good and it is sad that today very few people really believe in them and think the laws are just to stop them from living as they want. So we must remember to try to keep all God's laws as best as we can.

While Moses was up on the mountain with God, the people saw all the thunder and lightning. They were so afraid that they moved away and begged Moses to speak to them because they thought they would die if God spoke.

Moses told the people not to be afraid and Moses went into the thick darkness where God was. Besides the Ten Commandments, God's special agreement or covenant with the Israelites included many other laws covering all areas of their lives. When Moses returned he told the people everything that God had said to him. The people promised solemnly to obey all God's commands.

Then God called Moses up on Mount Sinai again. He

climbed up the mountain and a thick cloud covered it for six days. On the seventh day Moses went into the thick cloud after God had spoken to him and for forty days and nights the people didn't see Moses at all.

As we saw before the Israelites were all too impatient and quite likely to do something that would anger God. Sadly this is what happened again.

The people began to think that Moses was never coming back so they went to Aaron, who had been left in charge and said, 'Make us a god so that we can worship.' Aaron gave in to their pleas and made a golden calf from the melted down gold earrings of the people. Then he proclaimed that the next day was to be 'a feast to the Lord'. Aaron and the people meant to worship God by having this image in front of them.

So the next day they gave special offerings and ate a special meal. After this the people began to celebrate and enjoy themselves. What was so wrong about all this? The Israelites were worshipping the true God not a false one.

But the people seemed to have forgotten already the laws Moses had brought from God. They had been told that they were never to use anything that they made to worship God. God is our creator and so we cannot see him as we could see a golden calf. No matter how grand or beautiful a thing might be it cannot be compared to God so the Israelites were quite wrong to make a golden calf.

Back upon Mount Sinai, God knew very well what the Israelites were doing and was very angry that they had so quickly disobeyed him. God told Moses what was happening and Moses set off down the mountain carrying two stone tablets on which God had written his laws.

As he came nearer the camp Moses heard the sound of music and singing and then he saw the golden calf and the people dancing around it. He was so angry that he hurled the stone tablets to the ground, breaking them. Then he burned the golden calf and turned his anger on Aaron.

They have made them a molten calf, and have worshipped it . . .
(Exodus 32, v.8).

Moses' anger waxed hot, and he cast the tables out of his hands, and brake them beneath the mount. (Exodus 32, v.19).

Aaron could offer no real excuse and Moses had to make everyone realise how wrong they had been in making the golden calf.

Once again Moses returned to speak to God and to plead that God would forgive the people. He even asked that if God would not forgive them that God would look on Moses no longer as one of his people. But God knew that Moses had not done this wrong and so he punished only those who had sinned against him by allowing illness to come on the people.

God will only punish us for our own sins so we should not judge others because they will have to answer for themselves. Although our wrongdoing will be judged by God we can be sure that if we trust in Jesus, God will accept us. Jesus died for our sins because only he was fit to take the punishment given by God. No one else was able, not even Moses who was a very special servant of God. Moses was prepared to give up everything to save the Israelites showing how unselfish he was and how much he loved them. But God's love for us is far, far greater.

Moses enjoyed a nearness to God which very few people ever have. Although God is so great and powerful we read in Exodus, chapter 33, verse 11, these words; 'And the Lord spake unto Moses face to face, as a man speaketh unto his friend.' Some people say that even if there is a God he isn't interested in us, that he doesn't care about us as individuals. How wrong they are! The God who spoke to Moses as we might speak to a friend never changes. He is the same today as he was then and it pleases him if we speak to him in prayer. Moses knew what it was to be close to God and so can we if we trust in him and pray to him to guide us in our lives.

As Moses pleaded with God, he was reminded especially that in future the people were to guard against the sin that had just brought disaster on them. This sin is called idolatry which means putting anything or anyone in God's place. As nothing or no person can take God's place we should not use man-made articles even to help us to worship God. But we must also remember that we can make idols out of possessions or money or even famous people. That is also a form of idolatry. So God's warning to the Israelites of old is as relevant to us as ever.

God also told Moses to make two new stone tablets and after another forty days on the mountain Moses returned to the waiting Israelites. There was no sound of singing or dancing this time. But when Aaron and all the people saw Moses they were afraid to go near him.

What Moses did not know was that his face was shining because of his nearness to God on the mountain. So Moses called to them and Aaron and the leaders came nearer. Once the rest of the people saw Moses talking to these men they too came to Moses. So with a veil on his face Moses told them about all the laws that God had given to him.

God had given Moses instructions as to how to build what the Bible calls the tabernacle. The tabernacle was just really a big tent, used as we would use a church today. As the Israelites were always on the move the tent could easily be set up at each different camp. So Moses appointed two men, Bezaleel and Aholiab, who were very gifted craftsmen to work on the tabernacle and all its special furniture. They were also able to teach others so that the work could be done more quickly.

When all the work was done which took about seven months God spoke to Moses telling him to set up the tabernacle. So exactly a year after the Israelites had left Egypt the tabernacle was put up and a special service took place to mark the event. After all the ceremonies had taken place a cloud covered the tabernacle and Moses and the people knew that God had come into the tabernacle in a special way.

The cloud too was special, as from then on the Israelites knew when to travel on or when to stay where they were by seeing if the cloud had disappeared or not. If the cloud could not be seen over the tabernacle the whole camp journeyed on. But as long as it remained the camp did not move either.

The Israelites were very privileged in that God had promised to be with them at all times and in knowing his presence in the tabernacle. Nowadays we have many churches in our towns and cities but sadly very often only a few people go to worship God. We are able to worship God freely in this country but in some places people are not allowed to do so. They would be amazed to see how empty so many of our churches are.

We must not think that God can only be met in a church but if we are meeting in his name he has promised to be present. What a marvellous thought, to know that the God who has created this whole universe takes such an interest in us. If we trust in him he will lead us and guide us just as he led Moses and the Israelites. He is also pleased when we go to worship him and listen to the message of his Word, the Bible.

CHAPTER 6

On to Kadesh Barnea

The Israelites had now been camped around Mount Sinai for almost a year and perhaps some of them wondered if the cloud over the tabernacle would ever move. Several weeks had passed since the tabernacle had been put up. Others may have been quite happy as their life in a camp was sure to have been easier than when they were on the move.

But at last the cloud was gone and so the Israelites knew that they had to move as well. Each tribe and each family set off once more in an orderly way led by the ruling men and not as a great crowd of people rushing forward.

Moses spoke to his brother-in-law Hobab and asked him to go with them to guide them. Hobab knew the desert well and could tell Moses when they reached a good site for their camp. At first Hobab refused saying that he wanted to go back to his own land and his own people, but Moses managed to persuade him to stay with them.

So the Israelites travelled from Sinai to the desert area of Paran guided by the pillar of cloud. Once again the people began to grumble. They complained about only having manna to eat and of course all about the hardships they had to endure as they travelled on.

How quickly the Israelites had forgotten God's care and protection over them. He had brought them out of slavery in Egypt and now they wished they were back there. They had been starving without food and God had provided for them and now they complained about having no meat to eat. God had even told them that they were to be his special people, chosen by him and had shown them his power and greatness and yet the people continually disobeyed his laws. God was very patient indeed with the Israelites.

He is still patient with us today although we are just as likely to complain and just as ungrateful as were the Israelites. God has given us so many good things but how often do we thank him for them? Our homes, our families, everything we have is given to us by God. We ought to thank him for his goodness to us and should not hesitate to accept his most special gift which we can have through Jesus his son.

If we trust in Jesus we will have the gift of eternal life. When we leave this earth we will go to heaven to be with God for ever. God wants us all to be saved but only those who really trust in Jesus will live for ever.

Not only was God angry with the complaining Israelites but so was Moses. Even he became affected. He was so worried about his own weakness that he too began to complain. He was thinking that his task as leader of this mass of grumbling people was almost impossible.

'Why have I got to put up with these people?', he complained. 'How can I possibly provide them with meat to eat?' Moses was so unhappy he even asked God to kill him. We can see just how bad Moses was feeling to ask to be killed. But, thankfully God does not always give us what we ask for. He knows what will be best for us and he had plans for Moses to carry on as leader.

Moses' problem was that he had forgotten that it was not he who had protected and fed the Israelites but God who had done it. Only God was able to provide for all the needs of the people.

So, in order to make Moses' task a little easier, God instructed Moses to choose seventy of the leaders so that they could help Moses in his work. That took care of Moses' difficulties but what about all the Israelites crying out for meat to eat?

God certainly hadn't forgotten about them. They were

to eat meat for a whole month until they were sick of it because they had despised God by wishing they had stayed in Egypt. When Moses heard this he was a bit doubtful.

'There are 600,000 men and they will all have enough meat to eat for a month? Surely there aren't enough animals to provide all this food?'

Poor Moses had become like the other Israelites, soon forgetting the great miracles that God had done. A great flock of birds called quail appeared all round the camp and the people ate them greedily. They were so many quail that each person gathered huge amounts of food. In fact they spent two whole days storing up the dead quails.

What a great miracle God had performed for his people! Yet nothing is too hard for God. We should be careful that we never think that there are some things that God cannot do. Neither should we be surprised by all these wonderful miracles.

Although God can do all these marvellous things he is still very interested in each one of us. We can take even the smallest problem or worry in our lives to him and he will help us. If we ask him he can change our lives by his great power just as he changed the lives of Moses and many others.

Then, as if Moses did not have enough to do, being in charge of the Israelites, his own brother Aaron and his sister Miriam spoke out against him. They felt he had done wrong in marrying an Ethiopian woman and they were also jealous of his position as God's chosen leader.

'Hasn't God spoken through us, too?' they said. But God was angry with them because it was only with Moses that he had spoken as someone would speak to a friend. So he called suddenly to Moses, Aaron, and Miriam to come to the tabernacle.

There he spoke to Aaron and Miriam and asked why they had been so ready to criticise Moses. God was indeed angry as he had chosen Moses especially to lead the

And the people stood up . . . and they gathered the quails . . .
(Numbers 11, v.32).

Israelites. When God had finished speaking to them Miriam's body was covered with leprosy, a terrible disease.

By now Aaron had realised how wrong he and his sister had been in accusing Moses so he pleaded with Moses to speak to God on their behalf. Despite the wrong that they had done to Moses, he begged God to make Miriam better. Perhaps we might have felt that it served Miriam right but Moses had none of these unkind thoughts in his heart.

Nor was it because Moses boasted of his nearness to God that led Aaron and Miriam to speak out against him. The Bible says, 'Now the man Moses was very meek, above all the men which were on the face of the earth.' They had just been jealous of his importance.

Very often we are jealous of others, wishing we had their possessions or their abilities. We are quite wrong to think like this and we must ask God to help us not to be jealous. Being jealous is really saying that we are not content with what God has given us. Surely we can see how wrong that is. God does everything well and if we do not have the abilities that others have we must learn to accept this and believe that God planned it this way. We may have other abilities that we think are less important but perhaps others see it differently. We must accept what we are and what we have and be thankful to God for his goodness to us.

God healed Miriam of her leprosy but she was to remain outside the camp for seven days perhaps as a reminder to her of her foolishness. So until the seven days were up the Israelites stayed where they were.

The Israelites were now coming closer to the land of Canaan having reached a fertile place called Kadesh which was unknown to them and so Moses sent twelve men, one from each tribe, to spy out the land. He told them to find out as much as possible about the people, the towns in which they lived, and the land itself. They were also to bring back some of the fruits growing in Canaan. God had promised to give this land to the Israelites.

So the men set off and searched the land very carefully, not returning for forty days. With them they brought a big cluster of grapes and other fruits. Everyone gathered together to hear their report on the land of Canaan. Of the twelve who had been sent out only two, Joshua and Caleb, urged the people to enter the land. The other ten, while admitting that the land was fertile, said that the inhabitants were huge men living in strong, walled cities, and that they, the Israelites, couldn't possibly hope to overcome them.

Why were Joshua and Caleb so eager to enter Canaan? They, unlike the other ten men, were remembering that with God on their side they would be able to defeat any people no matter how big or strong they were.

But the people listened to the bad report and a great panic fell on them. As usual they turned again on Moses. 'Why have we been brought here to be killed by the men of Canaan? It would have been better to die in Egypt or even in the wilderness.' Then they decided to appoint a new leader to take them all the way back to Egypt, to a life of slavery.

Moses and Aaron were so afraid that they fell down before the raging people. Joshua and Caleb even tore their clothes because they were so angry at the lack of faith in God that the Israelites were showing. Again they reminded the people that God would help them to possess the land of Canaan. But the Israelites would not listen and were ready to stone them.

Then God spoke to Moses and told him of his great anger and how he would punish the people. None of them were to be allowed to enter the promised land of Canaan except Joshua and Caleb. For forty years they would have to wander in the desert until that whole generation had died. The ten spies who had given such bad reports died of

And they . . . cut down a branch with one cluster of grapes, and they bare it between two upon a staff, and they brought of the pomegranates, and of the figs. (Numbers 13, v.23).

a terrible illness.

This awful punishment shows us how wrong the Israelites had been. They had angered God previously but never had such a severe punishment come upon them. The people had shown no faith in God despite his promises to them nor had they shown any thankfulness for all that God had done for them. So now all those over twenty years old were never to enter the promised land. God told the Israelites to turn away from the border of Canaan and to go into the desert.

When Moses told the Israelites all that God had said they were very unhappy and mourned greatly. But instead of listening to what God had said they determined to try to enter Canaan. They knew how wrong they had been and how much they deserved their punishment and yet they were going to disobey God again.

Moses warned the people not to go because God would not be with them. He knew that if they went to battle with the people who lived in Canaan they would be badly defeated and many of them would be killed.

But stubbornly the Israelites marched off, determined to try to enter the land they had been so eager to flee from, leaving Moses behind. Perhaps they thought that if they showed their willingness to enter Canaan God would not punish them as he had said.

Disaster followed for the Israelites. The Amalekites and Canaanites who lived in the area attacked them and easily defeated them and chased after them as far as Hormah which was twenty miles north of Kadesh. How sad that the Israelites did not listen to Moses and obey God's command.

Much sadness will come upon us too if we disobey God and try to do as we please. He always knows what is best for us and works things out in keeping with his plans. We cannot know what lies ahead but God does. Surely it makes sense to trust in him to guide us. If only the poor

Then the Amalekites and the Canaanites smote them . . . even unto Hormah (Numbers 14, v.45).

Israelites had believed what Moses warned them of. God knew what would happen but the Israelites were too stubborn to listen.

Yet we should remember that even if we go wrong and do not listen to God he still loves us and will accept us if we are truly sorry for our wrongdoings and ask him to forgive us. Even the worst things that happen to us in our lives can be used by God to lead us to a closer trust in him. Then we will come to realise that he does know best and with his help will be more able to cope with any difficulties that we come across.

CHAPTER 7

Wilderness Wanderings

'But as for you, your carcases, they shall fall in this wilderness. And your children shall wander in the wilderness forty years . . .'

This was the terrible punishment the Israelites had brought on themselves by their continual disobedience to God's commands and their lack of faith in his power to bring them into the land which he had promised to give to them.

So instead of marching victoriously into Canaan the great host of the Israelites remained at Kadesh for many days. Then they journeyed by the Red Sea into the desert and moved from place to place. The many long years that followed gave the people the chance to realise their terrible mistake. But God still protected and cared for his people. Despite the length of time that the Israelites wandered in the desert their clothes did not wear through and amazingly they did not even suffer from sore feet.

God's miracles do not always need to be some extraordinary happening unconnected with day to day life. Imagine having to spend forty years either in a camp or tramping through a hot, dusty desert. We would soon wear out our shoes and our feet would become raw and blistered within a short time. Yet the Israelites wandered for forty years.

At least then the people didn't have too hard a time in the desert. Perhaps they realised that it was by God's power that they were able to survive and not on their own strength.

Naturally, because the Israelites were wandering for such a long time they came across hostile tribes and would have to learn to defend themselves. But all this was to prepare them for the day when they would enter the promised land. Some of the warriors would be killed in battle and so, those who had rebelled against God would die either of old age, illness or perhaps violently in battle. The young people would be growing up and would certainly be very fit and healthy because of their way of living.

It would be good to say that the Israelites had really learned their lesson and began to serve God humbly and obey him but sadly there were still those who were jealous of Moses and Aaron.

Such men were Korah, Dathan, Abiram and On. They gathered together a group of two hundred and fifty leaders, famous men, and came before Moses and Aaron.

'Why do you think you are able to tell us what to do? We are all as holy before God as you.'

When Moses heard this he replied, 'Tomorrow God will show who is holy and who he has chosen to do his work.'

The next day all the people were gathered together to see what would happen. Would God choose Moses or would Korah and the others be proved right in their belief that they were just as able as Moses and Aaron to do God's work?

God had specially chosen Moses and he was not going to allow others to try to take Moses' place. Once again God displayed his great power to all the Israelites.

Moses called all the people away from Korah and his followers and said, 'If these men die a natural death then God has not sent me. But if the earth opens up and swallows Korah and all his followers then you will know that God is angry and that I am his chosen servant.'

Just as Moses finished speaking these words the earth opened and Korah, his followers, all their families and possessions were destroyed as the ground swallowed them up. All the Israelites fled from that place, afraid that they too would perish.

And the earth opened her mouth and swallowed them up . . . (Numbers 16, v.32).

Once again the personal desires of one man, Korah, had led him to bring disaster not only on himself but on his family and his followers. He felt that it was wrong that Aaron was the man who carried out the special duties involved with the worship of God.

But God had given strict instructions as to who was to perform these duties and so Korah was really rebelling against God. By his power God made it very clear that Moses and Aaron were to carry on with the duties that he had given to them.

Maybe we feel tempted to think that God must surely be very cruel to allow all Korah's family to perish but we can never question what God does. He has made us so what right have we to think he was wrong to act in such a way.

We should remember that God loved us so much that he willingly gave his son Jesus so that those who believed in Jesus would enjoy eternal life. Jesus came to this earth and died a cruel death on the cross, suffering more than anyone else could ever endure, to save us from our sin. As the Son of God, Jesus had the power to rise from the dead, having taken our punishment. So we should never accuse God of being cruel or unjust.

But that is exactly what the Israelites did the very next day except once again they blamed Moses and Aaron for what had happened.

'You have killed the people of the Lord', they cried.

While all the people turned on Moses and Aaron they looked towards the tabernacle and the cloud was over it. Then they knew that God was there and they stopped their accusations.

Then God spoke to Moses. God was very angry at another show of rebellion and a terrible sickness immediately fell on the Israelites. Moses quickly told Aaron to take fire from the tabernacle and burn some special spices on it and then to hurry into the camp. There he stood between all the people who had died and those who were still alive and the plague stopped. But over fourteen thousand people had died.

How sad that after all these long years of wandering the Israelites still hadn't learned to trust completely in God. They still thought that they knew best and were all too ready to turn on Moses, God's choice of leader. What they so often forgot was that in standing against Moses they were also against God. Only when these terrible things happened to them did they realise their mistake. For some of them it was too late.

Many people today think that they know best and that they certainly don't need God to help them. How wrong these people are. We will never really be able to have a completely happy life without God being part of it. God created us so that we could glorify him and be with him for ever. But if we do not listen to his word in the Bible, nor believe in Jesus, his son, we will be rejected by God and will have to bear our own punishment. That punishment is far more awful than any the Israelites suffered. We will never be with God and all the good things that are ours in this life will be taken away. None of us can really want this so we must trust in Jesus and ask God to help us to live in a way that pleases him.

And Moses stripped Aaron of his garments and put them upon Eleazar his son . . . (Numbers 20, v.28).

CHAPTER 8

In Sight of the Promised Land

At last, after their many long years of journeying from place to place, the Israelite people reached Kadesh again. Here Miriam, Moses' sister died, one of the last of the generation who were never to enter the promised land of Canaan.

Although nearly all the older people had now died it seems that the younger generation were just like their parents. They had no water and so they complained again to Moses. God gave Moses and Aaron the power to perform another miracle and Moses struck a rock and water poured out.

But Moses had done wrong. God had specifically told him to speak to the rock in front of all the people. He was angry with Moses and Aaron for their disobedience. Moses had not given enough importance to the fact that it was God who had brought water from the rock. Their sin was punished severely. Neither of them were to be allowed to enter Canaan.

From Kadesh the Israelites moved to Mount Hor in the land of Edom. There God spoke to Moses and Aaron. They were to go up onto the mountain and take Eleazar, Aaron's son with them. Then Moses was to remove the special clothes that Aaron wore as the chief priest and to put them on Eleazar.

When Moses had done all this Aaron died there on the mountain and Moses and Eleazar returned to the camp. The people were very sad when they realised that Aaron was dead and for thirty days they mourned.

Once more the Israelites moved on, going by the Red Sea around the land of Edom. The king of Edom would not allow them to pass through his land so they had to make a long detour. This journey led the Israelites to complain again of the lack of food and water and of their hatred of the manna that God had provided for them. Their rebellion was so strong that they even 'spake against God'.

This time the Israelites had no excuse. They could not say that when they complained to Moses they hadn't meant to go against God. The Bible tells us quite clearly that they spoke out against God. It seems almost hard to believe that after so many years of special favour in God's sight that the Israelites could still be so unfaithful.

As we saw before God cannot just ignore sin. His punishment was to send 'serpents among the people, and they bit the people; and much of Israel died.' These serpents or snakes must have been very poisonous to kill so many people.

God takes no pleasure in punishment. He only does it to bring us closer to him and he wanted the Israelites of old to trust in him completely and to believe his wonderful promises to them. They could blame no-one except themselves for their misfortunes. By their own disobedience and failure to give God his proper place they brought punishment on themselves.

It is still the same for us today. We can never blame God for the unpleasant things that happen to us. The evil that is in our world is there because man disobeyed God not because God put it there.

But we should be thankful that God has provided a way to save us from the sin and evil that is inside us. His son Jesus said, 'I am the way, the truth and the life. No man cometh unto the Father, but by me.' If we trust in Jesus God will take us to heaven to live for ever. Jesus took our punishment so that we might receive this wonderful gift of eternal life from God.

When the Israelites realised how wrong they had been

they came to Moses and begged him to ask God to take away the poisonous snakes. 'We have sinned, for we have spoken against the Lord, and against thee; pray unto the Lord, that he take away the serpents from us.'

Moses had spoken to God many times on behalf of the Israelites but Moses now knew that he was never to enter the promised land. In a fit of temper he had sinned against God but hadn't he been provoked by the Israelites and their complaints? Perhaps if we had been in Moses' position we would have left the people to be bitten by the snakes. What about Moses? How did he take his punishment?

We read that 'Moses prayed for the people'. How unselfish Moses was. In spite of everything he continued to help the Israelites in whatever way he could. He didn't ignore their pleas and say, 'It serves them right', but went to God, who alone could take away the snakes.

God told Moses to make a brass snake and to set it on a pole and to go into the camp. Then if any of the people who had been bitten looked on the brass snake they would be cured of their sickness. Moses did as God had told him and it happened exactly as God said.

The brass snake itself was kept for many years to remind the Israelites of how God had saved his people in days gone by but sadly the people began almost to worship the brass snake itself rather than remember the God who had used it.

Even today people will go to see articles that are supposed to have religious importance but they too seem to forget the God who used the articles or gave other people the power to use them in a miraculous way.

Continuing their march the Israelites crossed over the stream Zered and then the river Arnon where they had to dig for water. Instead of grumbling and moaning this time the Israelites were happy and worked together to find water.

And Moses made a serpent of brass, and put it upon a pole . . .
(Numbers 21, v.9).

By now the people were close to the land of the Amorites. Sihon their king, would not let the Israelites travel through his land, and he led out his armies to fight. But God was on the side of the Israelites and the Amorites were defeated. Then followed another battle with Og, king of Bashan, and his armies. Again the Israelites were victorious.

This conquered land was so good that some of the Israelites asked to have it as their possession. Moses divided it between them but the warriors among them were to cross the river Jordan and help the other Israelites to win the land that God had promised to give them.

The huge camp of the Israelites now moved to the plains of Moab by the river Jordan. In sight on the other side of the river was the promised land. How glad the people must have been to see it at last. Perhaps Moses was a little sad because he knew he was never to enter it but as unselfishly as ever he carried on with his great job of leading the Israelites. One final battle was fought under Moses' leadership against the Midianites who were easily defeated. The way was now clear for the Israelites to cross the river Jordan and enter the promised land of Canaan.

The years of wandering had come to an end and God now called on Moses to hand over the leadership to Joshua, the son of Nun. Joshua was one of the only two men who had urged the Israelites to enter Canaan many years before, but his good advice had been ignored. Along with Moses and Caleb, Joshua was the third survivor of the Exodus from Egypt.

God told Moses to appoint Joshua as leader in the presence of Eleazar the priest and in front of all the people. Then they would know that Joshua, like Moses, was God's choice as leader. Just as they had followed Moses so would they follow Joshua.

Joshua was a very suitable choice. He was brave, and had already led the Israelites in battle but far more importantly he had great faith in God. God sees right inside us and no matter how impressive we might be on the outside God doesn't look at that, he wants to see if we are trusting him in our hearts. That is far more important than outward appearances.

So Moses' great task as leader of the Israelites was nearly finished. For many years he had carried out his work unselfishly, pleading with God on several occasions not to punish the Israelites as they deserved. He had been a skilful leader but had never boasted about his achievements. Moses knew that God had helped him to carry out his duties.

Our task in life is unlikely to be as difficult as the one given to Moses. But we can be sure that if we trust in God, we will be given the strength to overcome any problems and difficulties that we may have to face.

CHAPTER 9

Moses' Last Days

Before his death, Moses made a great speech to all the assembled people. In it he spoke of the history of the Israelites, including all their disobedience to God but Moses was really praising God. God had cared for his people and had continually shown them his power, his holiness, and his goodness. The Israelites had often needed reminded of this throughout their long years of wandering. Moses was giving them a final reminder that if they trusted in God and kept his laws faithfully they would remain as God's special people.

After this song, as it is known, came Moses' blessing on each tribe of Israel. One by one the twelve tribes of the Israelites heard Moses' words to them. At the end of the blessing we read 'Happy art thou, O Israel: who is like unto thee, O people saved by the Lord . . .'. The Israelites had indeed much to be happy about. God had certainly saved them on many occasions and now he had brought the Israelites to the land he had promised to give them.

We too can know this true happiness but it will only be ours if we trust God. Without him we will never be truly happy. Some of the unhappiest people in the world are those who are very rich or famous, with many possessions. How do we know this? They have said so themselves. These people have not had any time for God in their lives and so we must remember that having God as our Father, and trusting in him, are far better than having lots of money or possessions.

Just as Aaron, Moses' brother, died on a mountain top now Moses was to go up on Mount Nebo where he would die. There God showed to him all the promised land.

And Moses went and spake these words unto all Israel. (Deuteronomy 31, v.1).

Moses must surely have wished that he too would soon be entering Canaan but he knew that it was not in God's plan for him. He had prayed to be allowed at least to see the promised land and now from the mountain top he was able to see it stretching away in the distance.

Moses knew that he would soon be in heaven with God and he knew that this would be far better than even going into the land of Canaan. He had trusted in God and believed that God's great plan of salvation included him.

There on Mount Nebo, in the land of Moab, Moses died. He was one hundred and twenty years old but he was still as fit as ever. Usually when someone dies their relatives take the body and bury it but Moses was buried by God himself in a place that has never been discovered. We can see how close Moses had been to God that God buried him. God had chosen to give this great honour to his faithful servant Moses.

'And there arose not a prophet since in Israel like unto Moses, whom the Lord knew face to face.'

So Moses' life ended. He had been a general, a lawgiver, a judge, a priest, a prophet, and a statesman; all in one person. He had made the Israelites into a great nation, rescuing them from the cruel slavery of the Egyptians, and leading them wisely over many years.

We saw many times how unselfish Moses was. He showed no desire to have great possessions but was prepared to give up all his worldly goods to serve God as leader of the Israelites. He had never boasted of his abilities or of his closeness to God. In spite of the sins that the people committed he also remained very patient. God gave Moses the strength to be patient and keep his temper because he was not naturally patient. Remember how as a young man he had been so angry with an Egyptian that he had killed him and hidden the body.

How had Moses been able to carry out his task so well? The answer lay in his closeness to God. His great faith in

And Moses went up . . . unto the mountain of Nebo . . . And the Lord shewed him all the land . . . (Deuteronomy 34, v.1).

God's power helped him to go on with his work. He knew that he couldn't manage on his own but he also knew that with God on his side he would be able to be a good leader.

There is a verse in the New Testament in which God says, '. . . my strength is made perfect in weakness.' Usually when we think of strength and weakness we think of them as being opposites like black and white, high and low. So what is God saying?

The verse is teaching us a lesson that Moses had learned and which we would do well to learn for ourselves. When we realise that we need help in our lives we are admitting our own weakness. When we do this God's strength can be our help. But we must come to God and tell him about our wrongdoings and weaknesses. Moses knew this and so when he felt weak and unable to carry on he could rely on God's strength.

God also used Moses to teach the Israelites how to serve and worship him. Through Moses God gave us the Ten Commandments as rules to guide our lives. The Israelites were taught that God was the only true God and had chosen them to be his special people. He had a personal interest in them and would bless them greatly, providing for them and protecting them. But if they broke his laws they would be punished. If someone did something wrong they had really sinned against God as he had made the laws.

That is still true today. When we do wrong it is God's laws we are breaking. We should always remember this and then perhaps we would be less likely to do wrong.

We do not know how all the Israelites felt as they watched Moses climb up Mount Nebo and disappear from view. The man who had led them for so long was never to be seen again and they knew that on the mountain Moses would die. Their great sadness at his death led them to mourn for many days. 'And the children of Israel wept for Moses in the plains of Moab thirty days.'

Although the Israelites were never to see Moses again,
some others saw him many hundreds of years later and in
our last chapter we will look at this amazing event.

CHAPTER 10

Moses with Jesus

Perhaps we might think that 'Moses with Jesus' is a very strange title for our last chapter. Moses lived hundreds of years before Jesus so how could they be together? It is true that Moses is with Jesus in heaven but for the present we are talking about the story that is told in the Gospel of Matthew, in the opening verses of chapter 17.

Jesus took Peter, James, and John up on a high mountain and there he was transfigured before them. 'Transfigured' means that the outward appearance of Jesus changed in a way that showed his disciples his greatness. The Bible tells us that Jesus' face shone like the sun and his clothes became a brilliant white.

Then Moses and Elijah, a very important prophet, appeared and spoke with Jesus. A bright cloud then overshadowed them and a voice proclaimed Jesus as the Son of God and commanded the disciples to listen to him.

Why had Moses appeared? Moses represented the Law, which God had given him on Mount Sinai and his appearance was to show that Jesus had now come in fulfillment of all the prophecies and that now men had to come to God through Jesus and not by merely keeping the law.

The transfiguration may seem hard to understand but it teaches us that God wants us to trust only in Jesus. Many of the Jews in Jesus' time thought that by keeping the law very strictly God would accept them. Moses, who had been given the law, appeared with Jesus to show his disagreement with this thinking and that he believed the voice proclaiming Jesus as the Son of God.

We have looked closely at Moses life, right from his birth to his death and we can see many similarities between his life and the life of Jesus. These parallels, as we call them, show us why Moses is often referred to as a type of Christ. However we must remember that Moses was only a man and could not save us from our wrongdoing but Jesus is the Son of God and by giving up his life he took our punishment so that we can enjoy a right relationship with God.

Let us look more closely at these similarities between Jesus and Moses.

Firstly they were both protected as little children. We saw in the opening chapter how Moses was hidden in a little basket by the banks of the Nile to save him from being killed by Pharaoh. Jesus too was taken away by his parents to Egypt because Joseph, his father, was told by an angel that King Herod would try to kill Jesus. In fact Herod had all the children under two years old in the Bethlehem area killed so if Jesus hadn't been taken away to Egypt the same would have happened to him. In Moses' day Pharaoh had all the Hebrew baby boys drowned in the river Nile.

So even from their earliest days God dealt with Moses and Jesus in such a way that they were protected from danger. Two powerful kings wanted them killed but God protected two little children from evil. If God is on our side we can always be confident that nothing will happen to us that is not in God's plan. But if we oppose God we will find that even if we became the most powerful leader on earth we will have no real satisfaction or lasting happiness.

A second parallel is seen in the struggle between Moses and Pharaoh's magicians and Jesus' battle with Satan. Pharaoh's magicians were evil men but they were able to do exactly as Moses and Aaron had done except that the snakes they conjured up were eaten by the snake that Aaron's staff had been turned into.

In Jesus' case, he had to battle with Satan himself, the

one who had enabled the sorcerers in Egypt to do their work. But as the Son of God, Jesus was able to overcome Satan, despite the strength of the temptations. By trusting in Jesus and relying on him we too will be able to defeat Satan.

Nowadays people will laugh at the very idea of there being a devil but Jesus, the Son of God, certainly believed that Satan, or the devil, was real so shouldn't we? The devil will be delighted if we don't believe he exists and uses this lie to deceive many people. Don't listen to this lie. Remember that Jesus did not laugh at the reality of Satan but overcame him so that we too might be free from the awful effects of sin.

Fasting is not something that many people do today and probably very few of us feel that we could manage for even one day without food but amazingly Moses and Jesus both fasted for forty days. How did they survive? They survived because they trusted in God to give them the strength their bodies needed.

God may not require us to go without food or water for forty days but if we believe in him we can rely on him to supply all our needs.

Both Moses and Jesus performed miracles. They both controlled the sea and also fed a great crowd of people.

Moses stretched out his hand over the sea and God sent a strong wind which made a passage of dry land with the sea on either side. Jesus was woken up by his disciples during a fierce storm at sea and when he had spoken to the wind and the sea a great calm fell on the sea and the wind disappeared.

We all know the story of the feeding of the five thousand when Jesus fed this large crowd with five loaves and two fishes. Not only were the people fed but there were twelve baskets of leftovers.

When the Israelites grumbled to Moses about having no food they were given what they called manna, so that they would no longer be hungry.

We must remember, of course, that it was by God's power that these miraculous events happened. God is able to do anything including things that are far beyond our understanding. But we should never disbelieve any of these miracles even though we cannot fully understand them.

The greatest miracle of all is that God sent his son Jesus to die on the cross for our sins and that Jesus rose again and now we can look on God as our Father if we believe in his son, Jesus.

At the beginning of this chapter we looked at the transfiguration of Jesus and Moses' appearance with him. We also noted that in the Bible it says Jesus' face shone like the sun. The Bible also tells us how Moses' face shone too after he had been with God on Mount Sinai. The people were so afraid that Moses had to put a veil on his face.

Although there are all these similarities and others between Moses and Jesus, and although next to Jesus, Moses is possibly the most important person in the Bible there is one great difference between them. Moses was a human being but Jesus was the only Son of God.

Moses was a very good man but even he did wrong. He killed an Egyptian. In a rage he threw down the stone tablets. Again in a fit of temper he failed to give God his proper place.

But Jesus never did anything wrong at all. As he was perfect he was able to take God's punishment for the sins of his people from the beginning of the world to its end. Man had rebelled against God and sin and evil came into the world but God loved the world so much that he sent Jesus to die for our sins.

Moses was not good enough to die for our sins. Nor was anyone else. But Jesus was and in fact he died for Moses' sin as well as for ours. Although Moses never read about Jesus as we can he believed that God had a plan of salvation and Moses is with God in heaven because he believed in God's promises.

These things may seem very hard to understand but God has told us in his Word, the Bible, of his plan of salvation. We can be sure that they are true because God cannot lie so we must put our trust in Jesus and we too will go to heaven when we die. But we must come to Jesus in faith. God does not want anyone to be punished eternally but if we pay no attention to his offer of salvation he must punish us.

With God's help and guidance Moses was able to carry out a very difficult task. We too can be sure that the same God will lead and guide us in our own lives if we believe and trust in him.

Why did Pharoah want to kill Moses?

What country did Moses escape too?

What happened @ the well in Midean?

How many girls were there at the well?

What did Moses do to help them?

The name of the father of these girls was what?

What was the name of the daughter that Moses married?

What job did Moses have?

What amazing sight did he see while tending the sheep?

Who spoke to Moses.

What did God say Moses should do?

What excuse did Moses make with regards to speaking to Pharoah?

Who was to help Moses?

What was Moses able to do with his staff?

Could the Egyptian magicians do this?

What did Moses snake do?

What did Moses & Aaron say to Pharoah?

What did Pharoah say in response?
(Who is God that I should worship him?)

What did Pharoah order which would make the Hebrews work harder?

Who did the Hebrews blame?

What was the 1st plague (blood)

What was the next plague (frogs)

What was the third " (gnats) Gnats or Lice

What was the 4th " (Egyptian animals died) Flies

What was the 5th plague (boils. Egyptian animals died